The Library of Intergenerational Learning

Native Americans

Seminole Children and Elders Talk Together

E. Barrie Kavasch

The Rosen Publishing Group's
PowerKids Press™
New York

Our respect and gratitude to the Seminole tribe of Florida and Oklahoma —to their people and their future!
Sho Naa Bish (Thank you)

Published in 1999 by The Rosen Publishing Group, Inc.
29 East 21st Street, New York, NY 10010

Copyright © 1999 by The Rosen Publishing Group, Inc.

First Edition

Book Design: Danielle Primiceri

Photo Credits: Cover and all inside photos by JJ Foxx/NYC.

Kavasch, E. Barrie.
        Seminole children and elders talk together/by E. Barrie Kavasch.
            p.   cm.—(Library of intergenerational learning. Native Americans (Rosen Pub. Group's PowerKids Press))
        Summary: A child and older person of the Seminole Native American tribe of Florida talk about their history, culture, and festivals.
        ISBN 0-8239-5229-0
        1. Seminole Indians—Juvenile literature.2 Indians of North America—Florida—Juvenile literature.
        I. Title. II. Series.
        E99.S28K38 1997
        975.9'0044973—dc21   97-41100
                                                                                         CIP
                                                                                         AC

Manufactured in the United States of America

Contents

I Am Seminole

Tyler Harjochee is a Seminole Indian. He lives in Florida. Tyler was named "Little Mr. Seminole" for the yearly Seminole **festivals** (FES-tih-vulz). For these festivals, his grandmother sewed the **traditional** (truh-DISH-un-ul) clothes he would wear. These clothes show how his **ancestors** (AN-ses-terz) dressed long ago.

The Seminole people have five **reservations** (rez-er-VAY-shunz) in Florida, and more land in Texas and Oklahoma. Seminoles have lived on this land for a very long time.

Tyler wears his traditonal Seminole costume for celebrations and special occasions.

4

Our People: An Elder Speaks

"I am Max Osceola, Jr. I was named after my father, who was Bird **clan** (KLAN). I am Panther clan because that is my mother's clan. My parents taught me to respect my family, my tribe, and my education. My word is my bond. I represent our Hollywood tribe on the Seminole **Council** (KOWN-sil).

"Our tribe has been in Florida for hundreds of years. The world has changed around us. We have learned to live with some of these changes, but we always respect our old ways. There is a lot of pain and loss in our history, but we are proud of our traditions."

Max wears the symbol of his clan on his arm and on his clothing. ▶

Clans

Seminole children **inherit** (in-HAYR-it) the clan of their mother. Just like Max, Tyler is Panther clan. More than half of today's Seminole tribe of Florida belongs to the Panther clan. There were once more than twenty clans. Now there are eight Seminole clans in Florida. They are the Panther, Bear, Deer, Snake, Otter, Bird, Wind, and Bigtown clans. Each clan is made up of families who share common ancestors.

Clan **symbols** (SIM-bulz) are very important. These symbols can be seen in their patchwork sewing and artwork. The Seminole people wear their proud traditions when they wear clothes with these symbols on them.

Clan symbols are often sewn into Seminole jackets, skirts, and quilts. Here you can see the alligator and deer symbols.

Examples of colorful patchwork can be seen in Seminole crafts.

7

Celebrations

The Seminole people **celebrate** (SEL-eh-brayt) many things in life. God, nature, and the spirits of their ancestors are **honored** (ON-erd) in their celebrations. Special costumes are worn and dances are performed. The Seminole fairs, **powwows** (POW-wowz), and rodeos are big public celebrations where the Seminole ways are shared with others.

One activity that takes place at fairs is Seminole alligator **wrestling** (RES-ling).

Thomas Storm is a Tampa Seminole Indian whose father and grandfather were famous alligator wrestlers. Thomas is known as the last great deep-water alligator showman.

8

Alligator wrestling is popular with Seminole people of all ages.

Seminole men have been wrestling alligators for a long time. Alligators are big, dangerous animals, so wrestling with them can be risky. But men who wrestle with alligators today also teach their people about the alligators. They talk about their history and how to protect it. The wrestlers also talk about the many wild animals in Florida and why it is important to respect them.

Dancing plays a big part in Seminole celebrations. ▶

9

Elder Stories

The elders say that when this world was new, there was only one **language** (LANG-wij). All living things could understand each other and talk together. During this magical time, the Seminole **legends** (LEJ-endz) and stories developed. Some stories talk about where the Seminole came from.

"The Seminole stories teach us about nature. They also teach us about how to live and how we should act," Tyler says. "Some stories are almost like prayers. Others are very funny. A few are scary. My grandmother says that we should keep telling our stories to keep them alive. My favorite stories are the ghost stories. Sometimes my father tells me ghost stories at night after we eat."

◄ *Stories about the Seminole people are passed down through families and tribes by the elders.*

Our Lands: An Elder Speaks

"For many **generations** (jen-er-AY-shunz), our ancestors lived in camps near their farms and hunting areas," says Larry Frank, a member of the Seminole tribe. "Some families lived in **poverty** (POV-er-tee) near wherever they found work. Today, the Seminole Indians live on reservations all over the state of Florida. Our Big Cypress Seminole Indian Reservation is in the middle of Florida. Other reservations include the Immokalee and Brighton Reservations. The Tampa Seminole Reservation is near the Gulf Coast, and the Hollywood Seminole Reservation is near the Atlantic Coast. More than 1,550 Seminole Indians live on our five Florida reservations. Today we have more than 90,000 acres of land."

We have many cattle that like to graze on the flat land of our reservation. ▶

Families: An Elder Speaks

Sewing is an important Seminole tradition. Oneva Jones started sewing when she was young. Her mother and grandmother showed her how to make dolls, jackets, and dresses using their beautiful Seminole patchwork patterns. "Soon I was sewing my own pieces," she says. "Some of my designs show lightning zigzags, wind, or birds. This sewing helps honor our families and our clans by showing the designs and symbols that are important to us. Sewing is also something I can do with my family. My daughters have started sewing with me in the evenings, just like I did with my own mother. We like to sew together."

◀ *Oneva often sews with her daughters, Sheri, who is twelve, and Melanie, who is five.*

Festivals

"When I turned four I got to walk in the big Grand Entry parade at our Seminole Powwow," Tyler says. "It was a big celebration, and I was very excited!"

Thousands of people travel each year from all over the world to the four-day Seminole Festival and Powwow. The Seminole Honor Guard carries flags in the parade. The elders pray for respect and good health for their people. Everyone stands up and cheers for the people who fought in wars for the United States. The drums and singers make wonderful music. Indian dancers in colorful costumes swirl and dance to the powerful beats of the drum.

In this photo, Tyler walks with Suraiya Youngblood, or Junior Miss Seminole, and Vanessa Frank, or Miss ▶ Seminole, in the Grand Entry.

Food and Prayers

"Delicious warm fry bread with honey is my favorite food," says Tyler. "Fry bread is made at the festival, and I like to eat as much as I can! My dad likes his fry bread with lettuce, tomatoes, and cooked meat. We call this an Indian Taco." Fried frog's legs, alligator bits, or bite-sized pieces of white alligator tail meat, and sofkee, or roasted corn soup, can also be found at the festival. Tyler's favorite drink is a Seminole Smoothie, which is made from fresh-squeezed orange juice, lemon juice, sugar, and ice.

Special prayers bless the food that is eaten and those who gather and prepare the food. Seminole prayers always remember the children and the elders. The importance of each family is also honored.

Traditional Seminole foods are often cooked at Seminole festivals and powwows. In this picture, Loretta Micco makes pumpkin fry bread.

Language

Seminole means "runaways." This is because many of Tyler's ancestors ran away from the soldiers who tried to send them from their homeland to live in the West. Today, many Seminole people live in Texas, Oklahoma, and Florida.

No matter where the Seminole are, the importance of their native language is never forgotten. Chief James Billie, the chief of the Seminole people on Tyler's reservation, made up a song to help the children learn to count from one to ten in Seminole. Sound out these words just as they look. You can make a song of them too, just like Tyler and his friends do.

one	Thah me hen	three	Tou che chen	five	Chah key paun	seven	My younsh
two	Touk lee hen	four	Shee tee tah	six	E pah pah	eight	Kou lee Younsh
		nine	E yah wounsh	ten	Hah pook		

The Seminole language is actually two different languages: the Muscogee, or Creek language, and the Miccosukee language. The Seminole also speak English.

Chief James Billie likes to sing with his Western band at the powwows.

▼

Futures

There are many opportunities ahead for Tyler and the Seminole. Growing up here on Big Cypress Reservation, Seminole children are surrounded with love as they learn about their **heritage** (HEHR-ih-tej). Cowboys herd the cattle on large farms. There are **groves** (GROHVZ) of lemon trees and grapefruit trees on the reservations. Tyler and the Seminole always remember that these different kinds of skills—from alligator wrestling to sewing—are what make the Seminole people successful.

◀ *The future of the Seminole people lives in their children.*

Glossary

ancestor (AN-ses-ter) A member of your family who lived before you.

celebrate (SEL-eh-brayt) To enjoy a special time in honor of something.

clan (KLAN) A group of people who are related within a tribe.

council (KOWN-sil) A group of people chosen by a tribe to make laws for and be in charge of that tribe.

festival (FES-tih-vul) A day or special time of recognizing someone or something important.

generation (jen-er-AY-shun) All the people born at a certain time.

grove (GROHV) A group of trees standing together.

heritage (HEHR-ih-tej) The cultural traditions that are handed down from parent to child.

honor (ON-er) To show respect and admiration for someone.

inherit (in-HAYR-it) To get something from a person who has died.

language (LANG-wij) The words people speak.

legend (LEJ-end) A story that comes from the past.

poverty (POV-er-tee) Being poor.

powwow (POW-wow) A special Native American festival of events and gatherings.

reservation (rez-er-VAY-shun) An area of land set aside by the government for Native Americans to live on.

symbol (SIM-bul) An object or idea that stands for something else.

traditional (truh-DISH-un-ul) To do things the way that a group of people has done them for a long time.

wrestling (RES-ling) A sport in which a person tries to force a person or animal to the ground.

Index